AF377873

THE ESSENCE OF

911

UNFOLDED

CONT

ENT

THE
HISTO

ORY

1

FERDINAND PORSCHE

THE ARCHITECT OF AUTOMOTIVE EXCELLENCE

BORN IN 1875 IN MAFFERSDORF, Bohemia (today Vratislavice nad Nisou, Czech Republic), Ferdinand Porsche grew up surrounded by craftsmanship. Although his father hoped he would become a panel beater, Porsche was drawn instead to electricity and engineering. By age 13 he had installed an electric doorbell at home; by 16 he had wired the house with electric lighting—an extraordinary achievement at a time when most households still relied on candles and oil lamps.

IN 1893, PORSCHE MOVED to Vienna to work at Vereinigte Elektrizitätswerke while attending technical night classes. His breakthrough came at Jacob Lohner & Co., where he developed the revolutionary Lohner-Porsche electric car, unveiled at the 1900 Paris World Exposition. Featuring wheel-hub motors and no central drivetrain, the design was decades ahead of its time. The same year, he created the Lohner-Porsche Mixte—widely regarded as the world's first hybrid vehicle.

Porsche's growing reputation led him to Austro-Daimler in 1906, where he spent 17 years as chief designer. He developed high-performance road cars, military vehicles, and successful racing machines, including the 1910 Prince Henry Car and the lightweight "Sascha" sports car. The Sascha's class victory at the 1922 Targa Florio—and wins in 43 of 53 races—cemented Porsche's status as a pioneer of efficient, lightweight performance.

IN 1923, PORSCHE BECAME technical director at Daimler-Mo-
toren-Gesellschaft in Stuttgart. There, he helped create the iconic
Mercedes-Benz S, SS, and SSK models, among the most formidable
cars of the pre-war era. Yet increasing corporate constraints pushed
him to seek independence. After a brief and troubled period at Steyr,
Porsche took a decisive step toward shaping his own destiny: found-
ing an independent engineering company—laying the foundation for
one of the most influential automotive legacies in history.

WH-167678

"I CAME INTO THE WORLD AT THE SAME TIME AS THE AUTOMOBILE, IF YOU WILL."

FERDINAND PORSCHE

THE BIRTH OF PORSCHE MBH

IN 1931, FERDINAND PORSCHE founded his independent engineering office, Dr. Ing. h.c. F. Porsche GmbH, in Stuttgart. The company initially functioned as a consultancy rather than a manufacturer, developing advanced solutions for other automakers. Among its earliest triumphs was the Auto Union Type C Grand Prix car (1933), featuring a revolutionary mid-engine layout and a supercharged V16. The car dominated 1930s Grand Prix racing and foreshadowed the architecture of modern Formula 1 machines. AT THE SAME TIME, PORSCHE was commissioned by the German government to

REUTERS
Castrol
NSU
DELPHIN III
10
8
7
Auto Union Typ C
„Grand Prix"
1936/37

design an affordable "people's car." The result was the Volkswagen Beetle—destined to become one of the most produced automobiles in history. While its political origins remain controversial, the Beetle's technical influence on mass mobility is unquestionable.

During the mid-1930s, Porsche visited Henry Ford's factories in Detroit, studying large-scale industrial production at its source. He was impressed not only by the efficiency of the assembly lines, but by the structured, egalitarian workplace culture. Porsche returned to Germany convinced that true productivity stemmed from intelligent processes, standardization, and engineering-led efficiency—not longer hours. These lessons became central to his manufacturing philosophy.

War and Its Aftermath

With the outbreak of World War II, Porsche's firm became deeply involved in military development, creating vehicles such as the Kübelwagen and Schwimmwagen, as well as heavy armored prototypes. After the war, Ferdinand Porsche was arrested by French authorities and imprisoned for 22 months. During this period, his son Ferry Porsche assumed leadership of the company—setting the stage for the transformation of Porsche from an engineering office into a car manufacturer.

FERRY PORSCHE

THE BIRTH OF ICONS

WHILE FERDINAND PORSCHE remained imprisoned after the war, his son Ferry was quietly shaping a new future. He envisioned a sports car that felt alive—light, responsive, and deeply connected to its driver.

"It has always been a philosophy of our company that function and beauty are inseparable." — Ferry Porsche

The 356
A Vision Takes Shape

FERRY PORSCHE HAD GROWN UP driving agile European sports cars, yet after the war he owned only a modified Volkswagen. That humble machine led to a defining realization: a lightweight car with modest power delivers more joy than a heavy car with excess force. This idea would become Porsche's core philosophy.

In 1948, in a small workshop in Gmünd, Austria, Ferry and his team built the first Porsche 356. Using many Volkswagen components, including a rear-mounted air-cooled engine, the 356 was simple, elegant, and remarkably balanced. The aluminum-bodied 356/1 prototype was followed by steel-bodied production cars assembled in Stuttgart. A new sports car lineage had begun.

Ferdinand Porsche was released in 1947 and lived long enough to witness his son's achievement. In 1950, he made a final visit to Volkswagen in Wolfsburg before passing away in 1951 at age 75. The 356 quickly proved itself in competition, winning its first class victory in Innsbruck. By the end of production in 1965, more than 76,000 examples had been built. Yet Ferry knew Porsche's future depended on evolution.

The Story of the 911

"A GOOD IDEA is often surprisingly simple." — Butzi Porsche
Responsibility for the 356's successor fell to Ferry's son, Ferdinand
Alexander "Butzi" Porsche. Unlike his father and grandfather, Butzi
was a designer. His challenge: create a car that honored the 356's
spirit while surpassing it in every dimension.
Remarkably, Butzi had once been dismissed from the Ulm School
of Design. He would later shape some of Porsche's most important
cars, including the 904 race car—his personal favorite.
Under design chief Karl Rabe, Butzi rotated through engineering
departments, gaining a rare understanding of how body, engine, and
aerodynamics must coexist. His philosophy was clear:
"Form has to follow function." — Butzi Porsche
At a time when many car bodies were styled independently of their
mechanical reality, Porsche pursued integration. Butzi applied
this thinking to racing projects such as the Type 804 Formula One
car and the 904, whose chopped fastback roof reduced lift while
preserving aerodynamic efficiency. Design, at Porsche, no longer
decorated engineering—it expressed it.

Project 90I > 9II

BUTZI PLAYED A CENTRAL ROLE in shaping Porsche's next road car. Ferry wanted more space and usability, but without sacrificing driving engagement. Tensions arose when longtime design director Erwin Komenda altered Butzi's drawings without approval. Ferry intervened, taking his son's sketches directly to coachbuilder Reutter.

The result was Project 901: clean, compact, and perfectly proportioned. A long sloping roof, fastback silhouette, and subtly flared arches created a shape born entirely from purpose.

Unveiled at the 1963 Frankfurt Motor Show, the car was renamed 911 after Peugeot claimed rights to three-digit numbers with a central zero.

Production began in 1964. The 911 featured a rear-mounted six-cylinder boxer engine, delivering greater power, refinement, and balance than the 356. It was not merely a replacement—it was a new benchmark.

PORSCHE 912

Enduring Legacy

THE 911'S EARLY YEARS were not guaranteed success. Many loyal customers hesitated, prompting Porsche to launch the four-cylinder 912 as a bridge model. By the late 1960s, however, the 911 had firmly established itself as the definitive Porsche.

One final footnote: Porsche never officially sold a Speedster version of the last air-cooled 911 generation (993). Only two were built—one for Jerry Seinfeld, and one for Butzi Porsche himself, gifted on his 60th birthday. Butzi kept his car until his death in 2012—a quiet symbol of a designer whose vision shaped one of the most enduring forms in automotive history.

HOW THE 911 REDEFINED THE SPORTS CAR

BEFORE THE PORSCHE 911 debuted in 1963, the sports car arena was dominated by British, Italian, and American marques. Jaguar, Ferrari, and Aston Martin represented elegance and prestige, while Chevrolet's Corvette embodied American muscle. Most cars leaned toward either luxury or brute force—rarely both—and many were expensive, temperamental, and demanding.

The prevailing formula was front engine, rear-wheel drive, with long hoods and classic proportions. While effective, the layout often produced imperfect weight distribution and handling compromises. Truly versatile sports cars—equally suited to road and track—were rare.

Then Porsche offered a different answer.

A Radical Layout

Rather than follow convention, Porsche kept the rear-engine concept of the 356. Placing the engine behind the rear axle delivered exceptional traction and a distinct driving character. It was a bold decision that would define Porsche for generations.

Unveiled at the 1963 Frankfurt Motor Show, the 911 looked unlike anything else: compact, clean, and instantly recognizable. Its fastback roofline, round headlights, and taut proportions communicated purpose as clearly as elegance.

Performance with Practicality

The 911 introduced a new air-cooled six-cylinder boxer engine, replacing the 356's four-cylinder. Power increased, refinement improved, and the car gained a broader performance envelope. Lightweight construction and advanced suspension geometry gave the 911 remarkable balance.

Unlike many contemporaries, the 911 was designed to be driven every day. It offered a comfortable cabin, usable luggage space, and excellent long-distance manners—while remaining fully capable on track. This blend of performance and usability became a Porsche hallmark.

PORSCHE 911T

PORSCHE 904 CARRERA GTS

The Myth of the Widowmaker

Some 911s gained fearsome reputations, most famously the turbo-charged 930 of the mid-1970s. With massive power, short wheelbase, and abrupt turbo boost, it earned the nickname "Widowmaker." It could be unforgiving, yet that raw intensity only strengthened its legend. For many enthusiasts, danger and brilliance were inseparable.

Turning a Flaw into a Signature

The rear-engine layout was controversial. Critics warned of oversteer and instability, especially at the limit. Early 911s could indeed be demanding, but Porsche chose evolution over abandonment. Engineers refined suspension geometry, steering, tire widths, and weight distribution, gradually transforming challenge into character.

A turning point came with the 1973 911 Carrera RS 2.7 and its distinctive "ducktail" spoiler. Initially divisive, it reduced rear lift and improved high-speed stability. Track success quickly validated the design, and the ducktail became an icon.

What had once been questioned became celebrated: the 911 rewarded skill, precision, and commitment. Its handling demanded respect—but delivered unmatched feedback and involvement.

A New Definition

The 911 did not simply join the sports car establishment—it rewrote the rules. It proved that a sports car could be compact yet practical, demanding yet usable, refined yet visceral.

More than sixty years later, the formula endures. The 911 remains the benchmark not because it chased trends, but because Porsche had the conviction to define its own path.

turbo
PORSCHE
turbo

"PORSCHE... THERE IS NO SUBSTITUTE."

MOVIE STAR TOM CRUISE *in the movie Risky Business*

COL

THE
CARS

2

PORSCHE 901 (1964)

YEAR INTRODUCED *1964*   **ENGINE & CONFIGURATION** *2.0L air-cooled flat-6, rear-mounted*
POWER OUTPUT *130 Hp* **TOP SPEED** *210 km/h (130 mph)*   **NUMBERS BUILT** *82,000*
(early long-hood era combined)   **PRICE AT LAUNCH** *$6,500*

PORSCHE 901

The Shape That Chose Permanence

The 901 was not designed to shock. It was designed to endure.
 Long roofline, compact body, gentle curves — nothing decorative, nothing excessive. A form born from function, and confident enough to remain unchanged.
The rear-engine layout was already an act of defiance. Porsche did not pursue balance through convention. It pursued identity through conviction.

PORSCHE 901

Mechanical Honesty

Air-cooled, horizontally opposed, naturally aspirated. The engine's
placement defined everything that followed — traction, sound,
behavior, and challenge.

There is a clarity to the 901's construction. Metal is thin. Controls
are light. Feedback is immediate. Nothing hides what the car is
doing.

Petersen
AUTOMOTIVE MUSEUM

TYP 901

PORSCHE 901

Character Before Comfort

The 901 does not flatter its driver. It educates. It teaches weight transfer, throttle discipline, and mechanical sympathy. It rewards patience and punishes arrogance.

This was not a perfected sports car. It was a declared philosophy.

PORSCHE 911 CARRERA RS 2.7 (1972)

YEAR INTRODUCED *1972*   **ENGINE & CONFIGURATION** *2.7L air-cooled flat-6*   **POWER OUTPUT** *210 hp*
TOP SPEED *245 km/h (152 mph)*   **NUMBERS BUILT** *1,580*   **PRICE AT LAUNCH** *$10,000*

PORSCHE 911 CARRERA RS 2.7

Lightness as Weapon

The Carrera RS 2.7 was born from a singular conviction: weight
is the enemy. Porsche did not pursue dominance through excess
power or visual drama, but through subtraction. Every decision
surrounding the RS was guided by the belief that a lighter car speaks
more clearly to its driver, responds more faithfully, and moves with
greater purpose. The RS was not conceived as a special edition
in the modern sense, but as a focused tool shaped by motorsport
thinking and applied directly to the road.
Visually, the RS appears restrained, yet purposeful. Its most famous
feature, the ducktail rear spoiler, exists not as ornament but as consequence. Developed to reduce rear lift at speed, it represents one
of the earliest moments when aerodynamics were openly expressed
in a road-going Porsche. The bodywork remains clean and compact,
communicating intent without aggression. Nothing is decorative.
Everything serves motion.

nürburgring
Carrera RSR

Carrera RSR
nürburgring

PORSCHE 911 CARRERA RS 2.7

Engineering as Belief

Beneath the surface, the enlarged 2.7-liter flat-six delivers more than additional power. It offers sharper throttle response, stronger mid-range torque, and a more urgent character. Combined with extensive weight reduction — thinner body panels, lightweight glass, pared-back interior — the RS feels immediate and alert. The car reacts to inputs without delay, translating driver intention directly into movement.

PORSCHE 911 CARRERA RS 2.7

Emotion Before Rarity

Driving the RS 2.7 is not about spectacle. It is about clarity. Steering
communicates texture and load. Pedals convey resistance and
nuance. The car feels light on its feet, eager to change direction,
alive beneath the driver's hands. Emotionally, the RS represents
Porsche's purest expression of its core philosophy: performance
born from efficiency, connection born from simplicity. It is not a
celebration of excess, but of restraint — and in that restraint, it finds
greatness.

PORSCHE 911 TURBO (930) (1975)

YEAR INTRODUCED *1975*   **ENGINE & CONFIGURATION** *3.0L turbocharged air-cooled flat-6*
POWER OUTPUT *260 hp*   **TOP SPEED** *250 km/h (155 mph)*   **NUMBERS BUILT** *21,000*
PRICE AT LAUNCH *$25,000*

M · 7929 · IH
Hella
Hella

PORSCHE 911 TURBO (930)

Power Without Apology

The 911 Turbo was conceived at a moment when Porsche chose not to soften its ambitions. Turbocharging, still relatively new in road cars, promised extraordinary power but carried inherent complexity and unpredictability. Porsche embraced both. The result was not a gentle evolution of the 911, but a dramatic escalation of its character.

Visually, the 930 announces its intent more clearly than any 911 before it. Flared rear arches, wide tires, and a large rear wing give the car a planted, muscular stance. These elements are functional, born from necessity rather than style. The Turbo looks heavier, wider, and more serious because it is.

PORSCHE 911 TURBO (930)

Engineering as Confrontation

The turbocharged flat-six delivers its power in a way that feels theatrical by modern standards. Boost builds, pauses, and then arrives with force. This behavior defines the driving experience. Acceleration is not progressive; it is explosive. The rear-engine layout amplifies this sensation, loading the rear tires with traction while simultaneously demanding respect.

KRS 165N

PORSCHE 911 TURBO (930)

Emotion Before Comfort

Driving a 930 is an exercise in awareness. The steering grows light under power. The rear end feels alive. The car does not insulate its driver from consequence. Emotionally, the Turbo represents Porsche's willingness to offer a machine that does not protect its user from difficulty. It is intense, flawed, and unforgettable — a car that turned the 911 into a symbol of raw, uncompromising performance.

PORSCHE 911 (964) (1989)

YEAR INTRODUCED *1989*   ENGINE & CONFIGURATION *3.6L air-cooled flat-6* POWER OUTPUT *250 hp*
TOP SPEED *260 km/h (162 mph)*   NUMBERS BUILT *63,000*   PRICE AT LAUNCH *$65,000*

PORSCHE 911 (964)

Evolution Beneath the Surface

At first glance, the 964 appears conservative. Its silhouette is unmistakably 911, and that is precisely the point. Porsche chose continuity of form while quietly rebuilding almost everything beneath it. The 964 is a study in invisible progress.

The surfaces are smoother, the bumpers more integrated, yet the overall shape remains familiar. Porsche resisted visual reinvention, believing the 911's identity was already complete.

PORSCHE 911 (964)

Engineering as Transition

The 964 introduced technologies previously unseen in a 911: power steering, ABS, coil-spring suspension, and available all-wheel drive. These changes transformed the way the car behaved without transforming how it felt. The car became more stable, more predictable, and more usable, while preserving the essential rear-engine character.

PORSCHE 911 (964)

Emotion Before Modernity

Driving a 964 feels like standing between eras. It retains mechanical
presence — noise, vibration, feedback — but introduces a new layer
of civility. Emotionally, the 964 represents Porsche's first successful
attempt to modernize the 911 without diluting its soul. It proves
that evolution can occur quietly.

garde
A-GC.COM

PORSCHE 964 CARRERA RS (1992)

YEAR INTRODUCED *1992*   **ENGINE & CONFIGURATION** *3.6L air-cooled flat-6*   **POWER OUTPUT** *260 hp*
TOP SPEED *260 km/h (162 mph)*   **NUMBERS BUILT** *2,276*   **PRICE AT LAUNCH** *$85,000*

PORSCHE 964 CARRERA RS

Focus Restored

Where the standard 964 introduced refinement, the Carrera RS
removes it. The RS exists to reassert priorities. Comfort becomes
secondary. Sensation becomes primary.
Visually subtle yet mechanically purposeful, the RS sits lower, lighter, and tighter. It does not advertise aggression. It suggests intent.

PORSCHE 964 CARRERA RS

Engineering as Reduction

Weight-saving measures extend throughout the car: thinner glass,
minimal interior trim, reduced sound insulation. The engine
remains largely unchanged, but the overall experience shifts dramatically. Responses sharpen. Movements feel shorter. Everything
happens with less inertia.

Carrera RS
PORSCHE
L38A

PORSCHE 964 CARRERA RS

Emotion Before Convenience

The RS feels intimate and demanding. Road texture passes directly through the chassis. Noise enters freely. Emotionally, it represents Porsche's refusal to let progress erase difficulty. It exists for drivers who value involvement over ease.

PORSCHE 911 (993) (1994)

YEAR INTRODUCED *1994*   **ENGINE & CONFIGURATION** *3.6L air-cooled flat-6*
POWER OUTPUT *272 hp (later 285 hp)*   **TOP SPEED** *270 km/h (168 mph)*
NUMBERS BUILT *68,000*   **PRICE AT LAUNCH** *$65,000*

PORSCHE 911 (993)

The Final Air-Cooled Expression

The 993 feels complete. Not experimental. Not transitional. Complete.
Its surfaces are more fluid. Its stance more settled. It carries itself with
quiet confidence.

PORSCHE 911 (993)

Engineering as Maturity
Multi-link rear suspension finally resolves many of the handling
compromises inherent to the rear-engine layout. Power delivery
becomes smoother. Stability increases without muting character.

PORSCHE 911 (993)

Emotion Before Farewell

The 993 still vibrates, still sings, still smells of oil and metal. Yet it does so with refinement. Emotionally, it represents closure — the final chapter of air-cooled Porsche engineering. Not because it is perfect, but because it is finished.

PORSCHE 911 (996) (1999)

YEAR INTRODUCED *1999*   **ENGINE & CONFIGURATION** *3.4L water-cooled flat-6*   **POWER OUTPUT** *300 hp*
TOP SPEED *280 km/h (174 mph)*   **NUMBERS BUILT** *175,000*   **PRICE AT LAUNCH** *$70,000*

PORSCHE 911 (996)

Necessary Transformation
With the 996, Porsche crosses a line it can never recross. Water
replaces air.
It is not an aesthetic decision. It is not a nostalgic one. It is an
existential one.
The shape changes. The sound changes. The relationship between
engine and environment changes. For the first time, a 911 no longer
cools itself through air alone. The shift is immediate, visible, and
controversial.

Carrera 4
5-SKL-05

1 2 3
4 5 6
7 8 9
map
set
MAIN AUDIO SOUND DSC VOICE INFO TRIP NAVI
P
R
N
M D

PORSCHE 911 (996)

Engineering as Survival

Stricter emissions regulations, rising power demands, and global durability expectations render air-cooling insufficient. Water-cooling allows tighter tolerances, higher operating temperatures, and far greater thermal stability. It enables performance growth that air-cooling simply cannot sustain.

The new flat-six is smoother, more efficient, and significantly more powerful. The car accelerates harder, pulls longer, and tolerates sustained high loads without compromise. Objectively, it is superior.

PORSCHE 911 (996)

Emotion Before Acceptance

Yet emotionally, the 996 feels different. The mechanical texture
softens. The familiar air-cooled timbre disappears. The car becomes
more industrial, more controlled, more precise.
This discomfort is part of its significance.
The 996 exists so the 911 can continue to exist. It absorbs cultural
backlash in exchange for engineering longevity. It carries the bur-
den of progress.
In hindsight, the 996 is not a betrayal.
It is a sacrifice.

PORSCHE 911 (997) (2004)

YEAR INTRODUCED *2004*   **ENGINE & CONFIGURATION** *3.6L flat-6*   **POWER OUTPUT** *325 hp*
TOP SPEED *285 km/h (177 mph)*   **NUMBERS BUILT** *213,000*   **PRICE AT LAUNCH** *$72,000*

PORSCHE 911 (997)

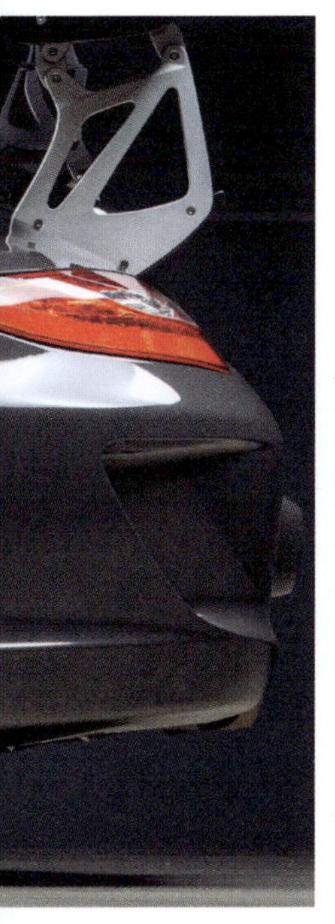

Harmony Restored

The 997 is reconciliation.
Not a reversal.
Not a retreat.
A refinement.
Porsche does not undo the technical direction of the 996. Instead,
it refines its expression. The proportions tighten. Round headlights
return. Surfaces become more cohesive. The car once again looks
like a 911 at first glance.

PORSCHE 911 (997)

Engineering as Balance

Power increases. Throttle response sharpens. Manual gearboxes
feel more mechanical. Steering gains weight and texture. Chassis
tuning becomes more communicative.

The 997 does not attempt to become raw again. It becomes honest.

PORSCHE 911 (997)

Emotion Before Numbers

Driving the 997 feels familiar in a way the 996 never quite did. The car communicates more clearly. It feels centered, resolved, confident in its identity.

It reconnects modern performance with emotional accessibility. The 997 reminds people why they fell in love with the 911 in the first place.

PORSCHE 911 (991) (2011)

YEAR INTRODUCED *2011*   **ENGINE & CONFIGURATION** *3.4L flat-6*   **POWER OUTPUT** *350 hp (combined)*
TOP SPEED *287 km/h (178 mph)*   **NUMBERS BUILT** *233,000*   **PRICE AT LAUNCH** *$82,000n*

PORSCHE 911 (991)

Precision Era

The 991 marks the moment the 911 becomes fundamentally modern.
It grows in size.
It stretches its wheelbase.
It adopts extensive aluminum construction.
The car no longer disguises its technological ambition.

PORSCHE 911 (991)

Engineering as Architecture

A new platform increases rigidity while reducing weight. The wider
track improves stability. Electric power steering replaces hydraulic
assistance. Electronic systems expand dramatically.
The result is a car capable of operating at limits once reserved for
racing machines — with effortless repeatability.

PORSCHE 911 (991)

Emotion Before Nostalgia

The 991 is not interested in recreating the past. It is interested in
outperforming it.
Mechanical conversation gives way to digital clarity. Feedback becomes cleaner, though less textured. Precision replaces rawness.
Emotionally, the 991 represents a philosophical shift. The 911 is no
longer primarily a mechanical object. It becomes a highly advanced
performance system shaped around a familiar silhouette.
It is less romantic.
It is more perfect.

PORSCHE 911 (992) (2019)

YEAR INTRODUCED *2019*   **ENGINE & CONFIGURATION** *3.0L twin-turbo flat-6*
POWER OUTPUT *379 hp*   **TOP SPEED** *308 km/h (191 mph)*   **NUMBERS BUILT** *Ongoing*
PRICE AT LAUNCH *$97,000*

PORSCHE 911 (992)

The Continuous Idea

The 992 does not attempt reinvention.
It assumes inevitability.
Everything grows: width, grip, computing power, structural complexity. The car becomes broader, lower, and more muscular, yet instantly recognizable as a 911.

PORSCHE 911 (992)

Engineering as Integration

Twin turbochargers, active aerodynamics, adaptive suspension,
rear-wheel steering, advanced driver assistance, and vast processing
capability operate seamlessly beneath the surface.
The car constantly measures, predicts, and adjusts.
Yet none of this is visible.

PORSCHE 911 (992)

Emotion Before Era

The 992 is the paradox of modern Porsche. It is more synthetic than
any previous 911 — yet easier to understand emotionally than many
high-tech sports cars.
It still responds faithfully to throttle.
It still squats under acceleration.
It still feels rear-engined.
The 992 proves that the 911 is not defined by cooling method, aspira-
tion, or technology.
It is defined by continuity of intention.

"THE 911 I BOUGHT IN 1992 CHANGED EVERYTHING FOR ME…"

MAGNUS WALKER *Fashion designer and car collector*

THE
BRAN

D3

PORSCHE 911 992 GT3 CUP

911 IN HOLLYWOOD

"IT'S $105,000 AND THIS HAPPENS to be one of the fastest production cars on the planet. Zero to sixty in four seconds. It's a limited edition!"

— Mike Lowrey (Will Smith), Bad Boys

From the silver screen to song lyrics and celebrity garages, Porsche has become more than transportation—it is shorthand for speed, success, and self-assurance. Few cars carry such immediate cultural recognition. Whether driven by movie stars, name-dropped by musicians, or collected by comedians, Porsche occupies a rare space where engineering excellence meets pop mythology.

Le Mans *(1971)*

Le Mans is less a conventional film than a cinematic document of endurance racing. Minimal dialogue, no romantic subplot, and an almost obsessive focus on realism define its tone. Steve McQueen, himself a devoted racer, partnered closely with Porsche to ensure authenticity.

The Porsche 911 appears not as decoration, but as part of the race ecosystem. In real Le Mans competition, 911s served as support vehicles, pace cars, and GT-class entrants. The film features a 911 S—2.2-liter, air-cooled, 180 horsepower—equally at home on road or track.

Legacy

McQueen owned an identical 911 S. It sold at auction in 2011 for $1.375 million. Much of the film's footage was shot during the actual 1970 race using real cars and drivers. While the Porsche 917 headlines the story, it is the relatable 911 that leaves the deeper impression: a race-bred machine that ordinary buyers could still aspire to own.

TAG
TAGHEUER
#D...ackUnderPressure
Gulf
Gulf
Gulf
Gulf
20

The Porsche in Bad Boys *(1995)*

Detective Mike Lowrey's 1994 Porsche 911 Turbo 3.6 is inseparable from the identity of Bad Boys. Wealthy, stylish, and fearless, Lowrey needed a car that projected precision rather than brute force. Director Michael Bay chose the 964 Turbo 3.6—one of the most exclusive and powerful 911 variants of its era.

Producing 360 horsepower, capable of 0–60 mph in four seconds and a top speed of 168 mph, the car was among the fastest production vehicles in the world. It also happened to be Bay's personal car. The 911 Turbo's duel with a Shelby Cobra on an airstrip became one of the film's defining sequences, cementing the Porsche as a 1990s performance icon. In 2022, the same car sold for $1.3 million at auction—far above the $60,000 Bay once received for it.

Later films briefly swapped Porsche for Ferrari, but by Bad Boys for Life (2020), the franchise returned to Porsche with a 992 Carrera 4S, and in Bad Boys: Ride or Die (2024), Lowrey graduates to a 992 Turbo S—650 horsepower and 0–60 mph in 2.7 seconds. The circle closes where it began: Turbo to Turbo.

BAD BOYS

Will Smith in front of the Porsche 964 Turbo from hit movie Bad Boys.

No Man's Land *(1987)*

If any film worships Porsches outright, it is No Man's Land. Charlie
Sheen's character steals only Porsches—not for profit, but for
passion. The film showcases an array of 911s in Coupe, Targa, and
Cabriolet form, with the 930 Turbo as the star.
Wide-bodied, turbocharged, and volatile, the 930 embodies the
film's dangerous glamour. One particularly memorable example is a
black slant-nose 930 with deep-dish wheels and aggressive stance—
an outlaw Porsche in pure 1980s form.
Here, Porsche is not status symbol.
It is obsession.

Gone in 60 Seconds *(2000)*

The first car stolen in Gone in 60 Seconds is nicknamed "Tina,"
presented as a Porsche 996 Carrera. In reality, it is a disguised 1978
911SC wearing a fiberglass 996-style body.
Smashing an actual new 996 through a showroom window was
too costly, so filmmakers transformed an older air-cooled chassis
instead. The result was lighter and more stunt-friendly than the real
car it impersonated.
It is a fitting irony: an old-school Porsche masquerading as a modern one, stealing the opening scene of a film about theft, speed, and
desire.

PORSCHE HEAD QUARTERS AT PORSCHEPLATZ IN STUTTGART-ZUFFENHAUSEN

PORSCHE'S BRAND AMBASSADORS

PORSCHE HAS ALWAYS stood for more than performance figures. It represents discipline, precision, and emotional connection. These values are reflected in a select group of brand ambassadors whose careers embody excellence across sport, competition, and culture.

Mark Webber *Motorsport Authority*

Former Formula 1 driver and World Endurance Champion Mark
Webber became a Porsche ambassador after retiring from racing in
2016. As a key driver and development contributor to the Porsche
919 Hybrid, Webber brings technical credibility and firsthand
insight into Porsche's modern racing success. He represents the
brand's deep-rooted motorsport DNA and its ongoing pursuit of
engineering perfection.

Emma Raducanu *A New Generation*

Grand Slam champion Emma Raducanu joined Porsche in 2022, bringing youthful energy and global influence. Her composure under pressure and rapid rise mirror Porsche's forward-looking mindset. Raducanu connects the brand with a younger, international audience while reinforcing its competitive spirit.

Paul Casey *Precision and Lifestyle*

British golfer Paul Casey represents Porsche within the world of professional golf, including the Porsche European Open. His blend of calm precision and competitive intensity aligns naturally with Porsche's values, bridging performance with luxury and lifestyle.

Angelique Kerber *Proven Excellence*
A multiple Grand Slam champion and former world No. 1, Angelique Kerber has represented Porsche since 2015. Closely associated with the Porsche Tennis Grand Prix, she embodies consistency, resilience, and longevity—qualities that closely reflect the enduring identity of the Porsche 911.

Sami Khedira *Leadership and Legacy*
World Cup winner Sami Khedira's role extends beyond brand representation. Through Porsche's "Turbo for Talents" initiative, he supports youth development and mentorship programs, highlighting Porsche's commitment to cultivating excellence from an early stage.

World Cup winner Sami Khedira's role extends beyond brand representation. Through Porsche's "Turbo for Talents" initiative, he supports youth development and mentorship programs, highlighting Porsche's commitment to cultivating excellence from an early

“PORSCHE IS ABOUT POSITION, ABOUT QUALITY, ABOUT PERFORMANCE, ABOUT ELEGANCE — ALL THE THINGS THAT I WANTED TO STAND FOR IN MY PROFESSIONAL CAREER.”

MARIA SHARAPOVA *Tennis star*

hollywood
AWARDS
RUBY RED
hollywood
AWARDS
ABSOLUT
RUBY RED
Nikon
UShot
hollywood
AWARDS
ABSOLUT
RUBY RED
Nikon
hot
wood
AWARDS
ABSOLUT
RUBY RED
Nikon

THE
END

4

THANK YOU, PORSCHE

PORSCHE HAS NEVER BEEN about chasing trends or reinventing itself for the sake of change. It has always been about refining an idea.
An idea that began with a small, rear-engined sports car and grew into one of the most enduring shapes in automotive history.

OVER THE DECADES, engines have moved from air to water, naturally aspirated to turbocharged, analog to digital. Power has increased. Speed has multiplied. Technology has transformed the experience. Yet the essence of the 911 has remained unmistakable: a car built around balance, feedback, and an intimate relationship between driver and machine.

The cars in this book matter not because they were the newest or the most advanced of their time. They matter because each represents a decision. A moment when Porsche chose continuity over fashion, evolution over reinvention, and engineering honesty over easy answers.

Porsche's story is not one of dramatic leaps, but of deliberate steps. From lightweight purity to turbocharged excess, from mechanical rawness to algorithmic precision, each generation adds a new layer without erasing the previous one.

What endures is not a specific engine layout or body shape, but a belief: that a sports car should communicate, challenge, and reward.

That driving should still feel personal.

That belief is Porsche's true legacy.

And, like the 911 itself, it continues—refined, but never replaced.

"I COULDN'T FIND THE SPORTS CAR OF MY DREAMS, SO I BUILT IT MYSELF."

FERDINAND PORSCHE

PROF·DR·JNG h·c·
FERDINAND
PORSCHE

CREDITS

Helmin Publishing would like to thank the following
for permission to use images in this book

2-3	JoshBryan	Shutterstock.com
8	Sergey Kohl	Shutterstock.com
9	Kittyfly	Shutterstock.com
10	Wojciech Wrzesien	Shutterstock.com
12	Giannis Papanikos	Shutterstock.com
17	JoshBryan	Shutterstock.com
18	ClassicCarPhoto	Shutterstock.com
19	Peter Kniez	Shutterstock.com
20-21	JoshBryan	Shutterstock.com
22	Markus Scheuerer	
5	Guido Bissatinni	Shutterstock.com
26	Stoqliq	Shutterstock.com
28-29	Serialone	Shutterstock.com
31	Featureflash Photo Agency	Shutterstock.com
34-35	Viktoria Kytt	Shutterstock.com
36	Joe Seer	Shutterstock.com
39	Joe Seer	Shutterstock.com
40-41	Tom Burnside	Alamy.com
42-43	JoshBryan	Shutterstock.com
45	JoshBryan	Shutterstock.com
46	JoshBryan	Shutterstock.com
48-49	JoshBryan	Shutterstock.com
50-51	FernandoV	Shutterstock.com
52	FernandoV	Shutterstock.com
55	Malcolm Haines	Alamy.com
56	George Trumpeter	Shutterstock.com
58-59	JoshBryan	Shutterstock.com
60	JoshBryan	Shutterstock.com
P62	JoshBryan	Shutterstock.com
64-65	JoshBryan	Shutterstock.com
66-67	JoshBryan	Shutterstock.com
68	JoshBryan	Shutterstock.com
70-71	JoshBryan	Shutterstock.com
72	JoshBryan	Shutterstock.com
74-75	JoshBryan	Shutterstock.com
76-77	JoshBryan	Shutterstock.com
78-79	JoshBryan	Shutterstock.com

81	Sport car hub	Shutterstock.com
82-83	elvisburger.27	Shutterstock.com
85	Niels Onderwater	Shutterstock.com
86	Roman Belogorodov	Shutterstock.com
88	Roman Belogorodov	Shutterstock.com
89	Audio und werbung	Shutterstock.com
90-91	JoshBryan	Shutterstock.com
92	JoshBryan	Shutterstock.com
93	JoshBryan	Shutterstock.com
94-95	JoshBryan	Shutterstock.com
96-97	Andriy Baidak	Shutterstock.com
98-99	JoshBryan	Shutterstock.com
101	Zuumy	Shutterstock.com
102-103	JoshBryan	Shutterstock.com
104	JoshBryan	Shutterstock.com
106-107	Veyron Photo	Shutterstock.com
108	JoshBryan	Shutterstock.com
110	GaboxProduction	Shutterstock.com
111	Brandon Woyshnis	Shutterstock.com
112	JoshBryan	Shutterstock.com
116	PACIFIC PRESS	Alamy.com
118	Tomas Vegh	Shutterstock.com
120	LB_06	Shutterstock.com
122	BFA	Alamy Stock Photo
124	Entertainment Pictures	Alamy Stock Photo
125	Entertainment Pictures	Alamy Stock Photo
126	Markus Mainka	Shutterstock.com
128	Jimmie48 Photography	Shutterstock.com
129	T Victor Velter	Shutterstock.com
129	B Masuti	Shutterstock.com
130	Jimmie48 Photography	Shutterstock.com
131	Celso Pupo	Shutterstock.com
133	s_bukley	Shutterstock.com
136		Shutterstock.com
139	Zuumy	Shutterstock.com
141	Edwin Stranner	Alamy.com

Helmin Publishing, 2026
Nivå Strandpark 2I, I
DK-2990 Nivå
Denmark

TEXT: Kelly Reising
DESIGN: butter am brot

ISBN: 97887-85374-25-7

Printet at Print Best, Estonia, 2026
I. edition, I. printing